IT'S A
JUNGLE
IN HERE

By Lisa Padrona and P. Joan Kent
Illustrated by Wanda Shigenaga

**An Official
Vice Presidents Anonymous**

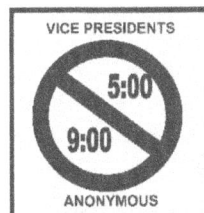

VICE PRESIDENTS
5:00
9:00
ANONYMOUS

Publication

Visit our website at www.StillwaterPress.com for more information.

First Stillwater River Publications Edition

Library of Congress Control Number: 2018943238

ISBN-13:978-1-946-30054-6
ISBN-10: 1-946-30054-3

1 2 3 4 5 6 7 8 9 10

Written by Lisa Padrona and P. Joan Kent
Illustrated by Wanda Shigenaga
Published by Stillwater River Publications, Pawtucket, RI, USA

Publisher's Cataloging-In-Publication Data
(Prepared by The Donohue Group, Inc.)

Names: Padrona, Lisa. | Kent, P. Joan. | Shigenaga, Wanda, illustrator.
Title: It's a jungle in here / by Lisa Padrona and P. Joan Kent ; illustrated by Wanda Shigenaga.
Description: First Stillwater River Publications edition. | Pawtucket, RI, USA : Stillwater River Publications, [2018] | "An Official Vice Presidents Anonymous Publication."
Identifiers: ISBN 9781946300546 | ISBN 1946300543
Subjects: LCSH: Chief executive officers--United States--Humor. | Corporate culture--United States--Humor. | Corporations, American--Employees--Humor. | Satire, American. | LCGFT: Humor.
Classification: LCC PN6231.E88 P34 2018 | DDC 818.602--dc23

The views and opinions expressed in this book are solely those of the authors and do not necessarily reflect the views and opinions of the publisher.

Contents

A good CEO:

- **Believes in the product**
- **Knows the troops**
- **Takes customers seriously**
- **Builds for the long term**

If you are reading this book, you don't work for him (or her).

Chances are your CEO resembles one of the all-too-common management geniuses who follow.

For your convenience, we provide dartboards with their pictures.

Office Dartboard Insert

Jim Fizz

He's the perfectly tailored, impeccably manicured silver-haired poobah, the kind you see in perfume and bourbon commercials.

Comes to work via company helicopter. He has his own floor, elevator, bathroom, and dining room with wine cellar and cordon bleu chef.

He buys a skybox at the stadium, a condo in Palm Springs, a bear-hunting lodge in Montana, a Formula One race car team, and a warehouse of modern sculptures. These are perks. They are deductible for tax purposes as a business expense.

Modus Operandi

Jim Fizz's first order of business is to initiate his state-of-the-art corporate strategy. He hires a world-renowned architect to design a new corporate headquarters that is taller than any building around. He builds the new corporate headquarters (which doubles occupancy expense), chooses and personally arranges the wall art, and streamlines the corporate name and logo—from Trans Recurrent Factotum Corporation, for example, to TRFCO. The cost of painting the name on the new Learjets exceeds the value of the property in the town where you live.

Once it's clear Jim Fizz is in town, he upgrades and expands the board of directors.

He recruits professionals who know the value of corporate expenses, like politicians, retired generals, and sports personalities.

He staffs up key departments like Investor Relations, Advertising, Premises, and Special Events. He joins every major business organization—the Council on Foreign Relations, American Enterprise Institute, Chamber of Commerce, and other organizations that get him photographed with important executives in New York and Washington.

Consequently, his work days are spent in the company jet, hopping from one press event to the next, and his evenings are spent at black-tie charity balls. Of course, this leaves little time for the business.

So, he delegates the business. He could delegate it to one senior executive. But he won't do that, because that person would be sure to engineer a coup. He could delegate it to two senior executives. But he won't do that either, because the board might side with one or the other and help the one they like to engineer a coup. No, what he does is delegate the responsibilities to a minimum of three executives, who will fight each other to the death to be his successor. Choosing sides will be impossible, since the third person will always side with the current loser. The carnage they initiate will convince the board that Jim Fizz is always the safest bet. Since Fizz doesn't know the business, he hires a world-class consulting firm to come up with the business strategy. After 12 months, the consultant tells him that productivity is off due to lack of production. This advice costs 5 million bucks.

Favorite Sayings

When the company's *earnings are increasing,* Fizz makes public statements like:

> "We are the Ralph Lauren of the gas business."

> "We are T - R - F - C - O!!"

He also makes private statements:

> "The bonus plan for the CEO doesn't adequately compensate for superior performance. Fix it."

When the company's *earnings are decreasing*, Fizz makes public statements like:

> "Our return on equity over the past 5 years exceeds the S&P 500 median."

> "A one-time charge for downsizing reduced earnings by $200 million. But earnings from core operations are up 30%. Core operations have been redefined this year as... "

In private, he says things like:

> "We lost 50 million bucks on a derivative? What in the hell is a derivative?"

When the company's earnings decrease, he has *to explain why*. This is what he tells the public:

"Interest rates did not cooperate."

"The competition from overseas is dumping product."

"Domestic competitors are irrational."

"The federal government increased taxes on inventory."

"We had weather this year. We had to close a plant for 5 days."

"The nation's economic turbulence hindered our industry's ability to compete."

"Our performance reflects concern over the continuing effects of the last worldwide recession."

In private he cites a different reason:

"Who sold us those diminutives—definitives—whatever the hell they are? Sue them."

Of course, investors will want him *to do something* about it. He'll tell them:

"The future is hard to predict."

"Economic and congressional uncertainties cloud the horizon."

"We will focus existing resources effectively on strategic initiatives."

"I will be staying past the normal retirement date to ensure that there is an orderly succession."

In private, he'll make other statements:

"Cut pensions and retiree medical benefits 50%, effective immediately."

"Enough of this price war crap! Get Brand X over here for lunch, and let's cut a deal on pricing!"

When the company's involved *in a scandal*, Fizz has to come clean in public:

"These allegations are preposterous!"

"We are unaware of any evidence of price-fixing."

"We are cooperating fully with the authorities."

"There was no wrongdoing."

"Vice CEO Blowfish has resigned to pursue other interests. Mr. Criscoh will take over as Vice CEO immediately."

He also makes statements in private:

"Price-fixing—my ass. Those jerks at DOJ think I can run a business without having Brand X over to lunch?

"So, what in the hell is wrong with that anyway?!"

"I'll tell you what's price-fixing: income taxes!"

Office Dartboard Insert

Chief Dumpling

When Jim Fizz retires for personal reasons, there aren't any competent people left to take over. He has fired them all.

The board of directors digs madly for an executive who has been around long enough to know what the company does and where the secrets are hidden. Also, somebody who hasn't made any enemies that anyone cares about, has no ideas that threaten them, and hates spending money. They'll tap Chief Dumpling.

He began his business career as deputy paymaster of a plant and worked his way into the comptroller's office at corporate headquarters. From there, Chief Dumpling transferred to positions in Auditing, Premises, Computing, OSHA Negotiation, Employee Benefits, and Personnel. Somewhere along the line, he spent a chunk of time upgrading information systems, but still can't use Skype.

Although Chief Dumpling belongs to organizations like the Rotary Club, the Knights of Columbus, and the International Order of Oddfellows, he doesn't attend any social functions. Between his 80-hour work week and televised ballgames, he doesn't have time. He mostly eats on the run. The one night a week he sits down for a meal, he goes to Denny's.

Modus Operandi

On his first day as CEO, Chief Dumpling disappears into the executive suite to determine his approach to authority and a vision for the company. He doesn't come out.

Chief Dumpling establishes his authority by implementing critical organizational decisions: outsourcing cafeteria services, revising the dental plan, and redesigning the telephone directory. The rest of the day he spends developing his vision for the company by reading back issues of the *Harvard Business Review*.

Favorite Sayings

Unlike Fizz, Chief Dumpling's favorite sayings are all communicated in writing.

In those few instances when the company's earnings are increasing, he lofts noble and luminous press releases into the commercial stratosphere:

"We are the leading edge."

"We manage change."

"We control quality."

"We control change."

"We control management."

"We search for excellence."

When the company's earnings are decreasing, he is sorely tasked with a response. His bewilderment shows in his press releases and in the scripts that he reads during calls with the stock analysts:

"Except for the losses in our core businesses, we would have shown increased earnings corporate-wide."

"We remain second to none in our core businesses."

"We will sell core businesses that do not perform."

"We will diversify into businesses that balance the economic cycles of our core businesses."

Dumpling will establish a corporate-wide strategic planning process to spur growth and profitability. To ensure the latest in corporate strategic-planning technology, this process will be guided by a world-class consulting firm, Drain, McBoozle, and Spray.

After 12 months, Drain, McBoozle, and Spray will deliver the strategic plan. The plan has a name—TotalNightVision 2020. It costs $8 million. But it is brilliant. It calls for cutting costs. And everyone knows it will succeed, because Drain, McBoozle, and Spray used the same plan at TRFCO's competitor, Brand X, 4 years ago, and their stock has gone through the roof.

To: **All Staff**
From: **Chief Dumpling, CEO**
Subject: **TotalNightVision 2020**

Effective immediately, all employees must pay for company time spent on personal calls. A form will be posted on the intranet.

In the spirit of Harvard's Delayering Strategy, effective immediately, all managers will work at a subordinate's desk 1 day each week. Pay scales will be adjusted downward accordingly.

During the transition period, employees are expected to be present on Saturdays. Officers who achieve divisional cost-cutting targets will be awarded one Saturday free per month.

Effective immediately, all senior vice presidents and above will attend a weekly motivational seminar facilitated by the Director of Personnel. It will be at 7 a.m. on Mondays.

You can tell the new TotalNightVision 2020 strategic plan isn't working when Chief Dumpling generates press releases like:

"We have the depth of management that enables us to meet the uncertainties and challenges ahead."

"We will be managing for strength."

"We will entertain any reasonable offer of a merger."

When things don't go well at a company, there is always a scandal involving money. Chief Dumpling is truly astounded when his company is caught in a scandal. Each day, he will provide a new announcement to the press:

"No TRFCO employee was involved."

"It was an isolated incident, implemented without aid, by an individual who is no longer with us."

"This subterfuge was a crucial factor in the loss of productivity and corporate morale."

"We are suing the individual involved for the full amount of the loss."

In private, he comes up with a new procedure to prevent future scandals:

To: **All Staff**
From: **Chief Dumpling, CEO**

Effective immediately, all expense requests must be approved by the next three higher executives prior to reimbursement.

It's a Jungle in Here

Office Dartboard Insert

Spector

Nobody ever sees him, but they know he's there. The PC logs show that someone tapped into the computers at 4 a.m. from a workstation in Easthampton, Vail, or the executive washroom on the 50th floor.

Who is the only person in the world with a master code to all computers? Who is the only person in the world who checks budgets from faraway places at 4 in the morning?

The guy the board brought in to enhance shareholder value after Chief Dumpling blows up. Your new CEO: Spector.

Spector joined the organization with impeccable credentials. He had enhanced shareholder value at six different companies in five different industries in the preceding 12 years. He's never had any production, sales, or managerial experience. But he knows accounting and bankruptcy law. Man, does he know them! He's got an MBA, a JD, and a CFA—and a system that works:

- Starve the company
- Pay dividends
- Carve the company
- Pay dividends
- Sell the "re-engineered pieces"
- Pay dividends
- Spray-paint the rubble
- Sell the rubble
- Pay dividends

Modus Operandi

At the earliest opportunity, Spector stacks the board of directors and executive suite with his personal friends: investment bankers, tax attorneys, private investigators, and accountants. They help him sell the cash drains. Sometimes, they own the partnerships that buy the cash drains. They buy the cash drains at what is called "fair market value."

Spector's next order of business is to reorganize. He fires all the top executives and writes off everything in sight. The massacre produces a staggering loss in the first quarter. The stock price goes into a free fall. That's when he buys all the stock he can find on the cheap.

The next order of business is to manage. He divides the company into cash cows and cash drains. Cash cows are divisions which require little investment, like making corn flakes. Cash drains are divisions that require considerable investment, like making cars. He sells the cash drains, milks the cash cows— and pays dividends.

For cash drains that are too lousy to sell, Spector takes a different tack. He turns them into cash cows. He:

- Cuts every expenditure that isn't essential to daily operation—like research and development, construction, repair, maintenance, and health benefits
- Delays every expenditure he can't actually cut—like electricity and security guards
- Produces a forecast that shows the division as a cash cow for the next 10 years based on the sudden improvement in profits
- Negotiates the sale of the business on an "as-is" basis

The division gets sold and goes bust within a year. This prompts lawsuits from the buyers.

But, as Spector intones:

"Hey! What did you do to it? It ran just great while I had it!"

When there's nothing left to cut, sell, or deplete, Spector goes on to the next higher level of strategic planning. Nothing enhances shareholder value as much as stock splits, rights offerings, spin-offs, lettered stock, and leveraged recapitalization. Spector can make more money overnight with a calculator and a copy machine than Apple or Exxon can make in a year. Never let it be said that you don't learn business in business school.

Sometimes the earnings of the company slip so much that even the accountants can't hide it. When that happens, Spector authorizes the company to borrow as much as possible from commercial banks. He takes the money and buys other companies. In the chaos that follows, no one can compute the bottom line, so no one can tell if it dropped.

Spector doesn't stick around to help the company pay off the banks. He moves on to his next CEO-ship just at the point where the deferred maintenance bills start coming due, the cash is fully depleted, the banks stop inviting him to

It's a Jungle in Here

lunch, and even the stock analysts have figured out how the accounting and legal tricks work.

Favorite Sayings

Spector never speaks to more than one person at a time. He doesn't want any witnesses. Of course, when the company's earnings are increasing, he's happy to talk with the stock analysts:

> "At $30 a share, the company is undervalued. We'll give serious consideration to any bid above $55 a share."

> "The company is going to buy back its own stock."

> "We're doubling the dividend."

In private, he speaks only to his lawyers and accountants:

> "Tell Morgan we'll sell the stock for $35 a share, take it or leave it."

> "Screw Morgan. Let's you and me buy 25,000 shares at $30. That gets in the news, and the stock goes to $45. If it doesn't get at least $40, we turn around and sell it to the employees for $60."

When earnings are decreasing, he keeps his comments to the stock analysts at a minimum:

> "Earnings aren't decreasing."

In private he tells his lawyers and accountants:

> "Sell the research and development team to Wall Street and lease it back."

> "Health Benefits! Can we cut them retroactively? Run the numbers back to January 1 and see how much we make up."

> "Okay, so go to monthly pay periods from weekly. We're not going to have a down quarter."

Then he tells his lawyers and accountants:

> "I told you to sell the losers by the end of the quarter at 1.5 times book value. You didn't. Get lost."

He's happy to tell the stock analysts what he'll do about "lackluster" earnings:

> "We keep only those businesses that produce an annual return of 25%."

In private he tells his lawyers:

> "Change the accountants."

When the company's involved in a scandal, he keeps his comments to the stock analysts brief:

> "Answering that question would constitute insider information, and we must protect our shareholders by observing the SEC regulations."

In private, he only talks to his private investigators:

> "Shred those transfers to the offshore holding company—now."

It's a Jungle in Here

ALL-STAR BOSSES

Your job is to do what the boss says. If you succeed, it is his/her accomplishment. If you fail, it is yours.

Reallocating credit and blame is a sign of superior executive talent. It is why your boss keeps getting promoted.

There are many different executives who demonstrate such talent.

The following are the top seven types to watch out for.

Office Dartboard Insert

Handicap

He's an overweight male with a perpetual grin, a drinking habit, a closet of tasseled loafers and blue blazers, and a stand-out preoccupation with golf, tennis, duck hunting, deep sea fishing, or any other sport that consumes time and achieves male bonding.

Handicap knows a lot:

- All the dates of all the major PGA, World Tennis, and yachting events.
- Most of the major players and how to imitate their backswings, forehands, and spikes after he's downed his second martini.
- The handicaps, tennis skills, and yacht types of all his customers.
- What everyone likes to drink.
- How to mix all the drinks.

What he doesn't know much about is business. Having filled up his head with all of this other critical data, there isn't any room left.

Modus Operandi

- Comes in at 10:30.
- Forwards all his emails to his subordinates at 10:35.
- Takes questions at 10:40.
- Drops names at 10:42.
- Visits his boss's office at 10:50.
- Drops names at 10:52.
- Goes to lunch at 11:00.
- Comes in the next day at 10:30.

Favorite Sayings

"Hey, uh Chuck, gotta meet with the Chief in two minutes. Can you fill me in on Project Alamo?"

"Just give me three important facts, Chaz. Don't want to confuse the Big Guy."

"Your evaluation? Didn't we just give you one? That was last year? Holy Cow! Well, schedule an appointment with Sally. She runs my calendar."

"Oh, I forgot to mention, uh, uh, buddy. The Chief wants more poop on Project Alamo. He doesn't think we're doing it right. I'll be out all next week, so why don't you fill him in on it?"

"I don't understand why we didn't get that deal. I've known Talbot for donkey's years. Sponsored him at the Mount Highsnott Yacht Club. I'll give him a call. Say, uh, Charlie, did you do something to piss him off?"

"Hey, Charles, dammit, the Chief says I gave him a bum steer on Project Alamo. What in the hell did you tell him? If there's one thing I can't stand, it's guys like you, who are paid to know what you're doing, screwing up things with the CEO."

"Hey, uh Chuck, gotta meet with the Chief in two minutes. Can you fill me in on Project Bonanza?"

Office Dartboard Insert

Dwight Debit

You were so thrilled to get a job when you started out, it didn't occur to you that you had 3 years of boot camp coming your way.

Modus Operandi

J. Dwight Debit is immediately identifiable in any company by his dress. You can spot him a mile away. He's the guy who is never casual. He's also the guy who prints everything out because he won't read text on a screen.

Because Debit is not very bright, he does everything by the book. It took him forever to get where he is. So, he's not going to let you get ahead any faster. He trips you up at every possible opportunity, mostly using rules from his book that are obscure or irrelevant.

Debit can't stand change because change is not in his book. If change gets forced down from the top, he's the first to disappear behind closed office doors. He'll stick you out front to manage it and, once he knows what the change is, do his best to sabotage it.

Favorite Sayings

"I watched you today. You made three personal phone calls. This must stop. Office hours are for working."

"This desk does not belong to you. It belongs to my division. You are in my division. Your desk is filthy! A pigsty. Clean it at once!"

"Do not email me. Emails tend to use abbreviations and have no respect for format. I will read only printed memos."

"Effective immediately, all memos from my division are to be 12-pitch type with margins as follows: top margin, one and one quarter inch; bottom margin, one inch; left margin, one and one half inch; right margin, one inch. This includes all memos that are to be reviewed by the undersigned. Memos that do not comply will not be reviewed."

"Exactly when did it become clear to you that leaving at 4:30 on the Wednesday before Thanksgiving is acceptable corporate conduct?"

"It used to be that managers started out in Operations. I spent 15 of my most formative years in Collections. An excellent introduction to this organization. You should have started out this way."

"I heard you on the call today with General International. You NEVER beg for the business with a client! They are lucky to be doing business with us! LUCKY!"

"Mr. Pendleton, you have done well. You're polished, and you're tidy. You have a fine rapport with our clients. Clearly, you share their backgrounds. That's been the key to my success with clients too."

"Miss Fittipaldi, you are pushy and tactless. You are always rushing around, upsetting the division strategy and schedule with your far-fetched ideas and unreasonable deadlines."

"It's chaos in the financial markets! They're letting just anyone in! Everybody is getting into everybody else's business. And nobody is doing any of it well. It's all downhill from here."

"Miss Fittipaldi, I don't care who's responsible for this mess. I insist that you fix it! Now!"

Office Dartboard Insert

Dick Dujour

Dick Dujour is the product of second-rate prep schools, where he honed his interpersonal skills to lethal efficiency over the 13 years he spent in them. He never answers a question. He never gets cornered. He attacks everything that moves—if it is at or below his level. He gets away with absolutely everything he does and says.

Modus Operandi

- Yells obscenities from across the room.
- Titters when anyone makes a mistake, gets sick, or has to go to a funeral.
- Responds to your emails with comments like: "Am I supposed to know what you are talking about?" "Does anybody know what you are talking about?" "Can you be serious?" "C'mon, you couldn't have spent more than 2 minutes on this." "My 2-year-old dog could do better than this."
- Goes through your desk when you're on vacation and takes whatever he wants.
- Throws out whatever he doesn't want, like your umbrella, spare pair of shoes, or photos of your kids—the ones he calls ugly.
- Phones you up on vacation to get answers instead of looking it up himself.
- Phones you up on vacation to tell you what a lousy job you did on a project.
- Leaves a message on your home voicemail that there's been a major reorganization that he'll tell you about when you get back. Doesn't answer his phone when you call back frantically.
- Talks to you on his speakerphone without letting you know who else is in the room.
- Threatens to fire you and "all of your ilk." Daily.

Favorite Sayings

"Jim is a cretin."

"John is an imbecile."

"Bill is a moron."

"Doris is tight with the boss. If you know what I mean."

"How are your customers? Do they know who you are?"

"What sort of last name is that anyway?"

"Where'd you go to college? ... Never heard of it."

"That's the most pathetic restaurant I've ever been to. Eat there often?"

"You call this finished?"

"There's nothing complicated about business. You either get it or you don't. You don't."

"I didn't say you'd get a 10% raise. I said it was *possible* to get a 10% raise—and it is! For some people."

"Today must be your day. You're wearing matching socks."

"You remind me of Jack. Of course, he's no longer with us."

"Have you ever considered working? Elsewhere?"

Office Dartboard Insert

Treadmill

Treadmill is convinced that the corporation is depending on him to do it *all,* and that he is up to the task. He loads up on all the latest electronic gadgets and sets up installations in his office, home, car, and briefcase. He never sits still; he bobs and weaves like a championship ping-pong player. He doesn't feel comfortable talking on fewer than two phones at a time. He drapes his desk in paper and half-eaten junk food. When trapped in his office, he paces, chews on pens, and gulps pints of coffee while talking. When forced to sit, he maintains productivity by doing three or four things simultaneously—surfing through emails, writing an evaluation, and shining his shoes. He keeps a complete change of clothes in a file cabinet, just in case he has to fly to Frankfurt on 2-hours' notice. Recreation involves things that don't take much time: squash, handball, or running on a treadmill. He doesn't approve of vacation or sick days, for himself or any of his subordinates.

Modus Operandi

- He emails a week-long assignment to you at 5 p.m. on Friday and demands it back on his desk—complete—by Monday at 6 a.m.
- He judges all his subordinates on the basis of how long they stay at the office.
- He fires off orders verbally and expects you to remember each detail.
- He never explains what he's said.
- He never remembers what he's said.

Favorite Sayings

"This is a department of winners."

"What do you mean he can't see us for *2 weeks?* That gives Brand X all the time in the world to get the business. You sit down right now and write a proposal. Gotta show him we're hungry!"

"We'll organize into teams. I want you to lead Red Team. Call your troops together and outline the tasks. Let's see, it's 15:00 hours now. I want a report back by 19:00 hours. I've already ordered pizza and Chinese."

"Nice job! Let's dialogue later! Gotta run!"

"Performance review? No can do. I'm leaving at 5 today. Half day. It's one of my basic rules: One night a week I get home before the kids go to bed. I stick to it."

"I was ready to give you your performance review last night. I looked around for you at 8 p.m., but you'd already gone home."

"I can't help it. No bonuses this year. Okay, so we'll have to do more with less. Think: CAN-DO!! We'll just start working smart."

Office Dartboard Insert

Den Mother

It's a Jungle in Here

Den Mother is the only boss who's nice and open and wants to be called by his childhood nickname. He is open and nice because he wants everyone else to be open and nice. The only subordinates he feels comfortable with are the ones who are open and nice. They are also the ones who are even less competent than he is, which is why he promotes them. The high point of your relationship with him occurs when one of your idiot subordinates gets promoted to your level and takes over your business territory. And you get sent off to monitor operations in the Bakersfield office. The day you depart, Den Mother will throw an office party and toast your talents with fruit punch in paper cups.

Modus Operandi

- Calls daily team meetings to resolve minor issues.
- Gets team votes on major issues.
- Does what he wants, regardless of how the team votes.
- Tells competent people that their performance is weak in those areas in which he himself is weakest.
- Makes all sorts of promises to competent subordinates.
- Doesn't keep any of them.

Den Mother never personally claims responsibility for a job well done. He always calls it a team effort. Since none of his subordinates is mentioned by name, his boss always thinks that Den Mother did it all anyway.

Favorite Sayings

"We're all in this together, and we've got to help each other out."

"I had lunch with your subordinates while you were on vacation. You haven't been giving them enough challenging work. So, I handed out some new assignments. Don't worry, I'll monitor their progress."

"I'm sorry. I just can't afford to have one manager getting half of the department's revenues and four managers getting the other half. It's just not good teamwork."

"Besides, reallocating your customers to them gives you more time to work on the things you need to improve—like administration."

"Listen, you're not the only one who's ever been passed over. It's happened to me many times, and you just can't take it personally. But you do need improvement in administration."

"You *are* my deputy. On Tuesdays and Thursdays. I just can't make it official."

"I've got a great promotion for you: Bakersfield!"

Office Dartboard Insert

Chicken Little

Here he comes, in his perpetual sweat, tie askew, nails chewed to the nubs, launching 180-degree scans of the floor at half-minute intervals. His voice quavers when he speaks with an audience of one or more people. Everything that happens is of equal importance. Everything is an absolute crisis. He hasn't learned the basic fact that 80% of what an executive does is trivial and wouldn't be missed if nobody did it. He can't learn this because he's convinced that he's being monitored by HR 24/7.

Modus Operandi

- He gives you an assignment, and an hour later, when you're halfway through it, he takes it back and gives you another one.
- A half-hour later, he takes the second one away and insists that you read the Procedure Manual concerning a third crisis that just came up.
- He amplifies everything his boss says, particularly bad things. When bad things are said, he calls a crisis meeting with all his subordinates.
- He constantly creates organizational charts to better handle the flow of random crises. There are always more slots on these charts than there are people in his department, so he often ends up reporting to himself in the chart.

Favorite Sayings

"I need your business projections by customer in the next 30 minutes!"

"You'd better check, double check, and triple check those figures. We can't afford a mistake."

"Nothing, but *nothing,* goes out of the division unless I've checked it first. Quality control is the basis of excellence!"

"Stop everything! Put down that phone! We've got to calculate depreciation on all the office furniture."

"You are taking supplies from the cabinet without filling out the form! Do you think Purchasing won't find out? You never, but *never*, want to run afoul of Purchasing!"

"Stop what you're doing! I said Stop! The Audit Department needs last month's travel expenses for a 10:30 meeting with the Big Boss! I said stop it *now*!"

Of course, Chicken Little is absolutely right about one thing: The sky really is falling.

Where he's wrong is that he thinks somebody cares.

Office Dartboard Insert

Wyatt Earp

It's a Jungle in Here

Wyatt Earp is probably the only boss you'll encounter who will personally fire you. He's being paid to come in and clean up a department that's missing budget. He has authority, as he clearly will tell you. You can also tell he has authority because he dresses in the latest power styles and carries the most desirable accessories: The Watch, The Bag, The Phone, The Hand-Made Shoes, and the Suspenders with funny pictures of unicorns, golf clubs, and trumpets. Of course, to lure him from Brand X, the company had to pay him twice as much money as any of the other bosses at his level. This gives him even more authority. And just in case anyone has missed the point, Wyatt fires two subordinates at random his first day at work.

Becoming the fastest gun on the floor is merely his short-term goal. Wyatt's long-term goal is to be a certified master of the universe, and he's going to do whatever he can to get there: run a team, get promoted, run a division, get promoted, run the company, become CEO, get stock options, give interviews, divorce his first wife, buy companies, marry a 20-year-old actress, and rise to the top of the Forbes 400. Anything that gets in the way of his trajectory—staff, boss, customers, kids, business—gets blown away.

Modus Operandi

- Encourages subordinates to criticize everything and everyone in the company.
- Records conversations.
- Repeats what he's been told in confidence.
- Encourages his subordinates to break all the rules they need to break to make budget.
- Lets subordinates take the heat when they get caught.
- Fires them because they got caught.
- Joins the same country club as the CEO.
- Plays golf with the CEO.
- Keeps the CEO up to date on the failures of everyone in the organization.
- Gets the dirt on the CEO's wife.
- Keeps board members and HR up to date on the CEO.
- Keeps the local media up to date on the progress of his career.

Favorite Sayings

"Doing business with customers is simple: You've got to just get out there and jump the suckers."

"Let me tell you how we learned to handle it at Wharton."

"There's only one way to turn this company around: Get rid of everyone."

"There's one other thing before you clear out your desk ..."

THE ALL-PRO COLLEAGUES

When you start out at a company, you are usually at the bottom of the organization chart. Everybody at the bottom of the organization chart is a buddy. That's because they can't fire each other. The camaraderie can last for up to a year.

For those who are left after the first year, everything changes. In order to stay, you have to move up the ladder. But at every rung there's less room. Somebody's got to fall off.

Your colleagues are there to help you fall off. Here are the ones who work hardest at helping you fall off.

Office Dartboard Insert

Deputy Tool

Who's that woman in the pinstriped suit and suspenders, racing up the corridor? Why it's your colleague, Victoria! Why's she racing? To catch up with her master—your mutual boss—who's on his way to the men's room. "I just phoned Sheldon Parsley to get an appointment for us on Tuesday. He was in a meeting. But his secretary said that he'd call back this afternoon."

While she escorts the boss back to his office, Victoria continues: "But if he can't do it, it's okay. I've got a back-up strategy. Instead of doing Chicago, we could do Des Moines and see Bennet Hasher. He often tells me in my daily call how much he'd like to see you again."

Who is this overgrown Teacher's Pet? Deputy Tool.

Modus Operandi

- Gives the boss all the dirt on you, your subordinates, and your other colleagues and their subordinates.
- Gives the boss dirt on the boss's colleagues.
- Does all the tasks the boss doesn't want to do.
- Takes the blame for the boss's minor mistakes.
- Signs the boss's expenses.

The boss will be delighted with all the help. In return for these reliable services, the boss does things for your colleague:

- Puts Deputy Tool in charge when he's out of the office.
- Puts Deputy Tool's name first in the email distribution list.
- Shows Deputy Tool's work to you and the rest of the colleagues as an example of how the work should be done.
- Gives her the best assignments.
- Gives her the best subordinates.
- Invites her to meetings with senior management.
- Goes out to lunch with her and nobody else.
- Lets her take vacation between Christmas and New Year's.

You can be doing ten times the business that Deputy Tool does, but it doesn't make any difference. As far as the division is concerned, Deputy Tool is *de facto* second in command, and you and the rest of your colleagues report to her.

Tool promotes this notion by limiting her contact with you and everyone else in the division below the level of the boss:

- Never answers anyone else's phone, unless it's the boss's.
- Never lets anyone use any of her resources: e.g., her share of the administrative assistant, her desk supplies, or the electrical sockets on her walls.
- Communicates with you and the rest of her colleagues only by email—so she's never seen talking with inferiors, and so she can blind copy the boss on her "team play."

And though she's not interested in talking with you, she's passionately interested in keeping the boss up to date on your performance:

"Pam's been yelling at her subordinates. Maybe she's having personal problems? Or could she still be struggling with her management skills?"

Nothing is more astonishing to Deputy Tool than seeing a colleague of hers get promoted. Tool takes other people's promotions as a personal affront.

"How could this happen? He's jumped two boxes in the org chart. And that's after he did such a miserable job on the Parsley account. Obviously, the boss didn't know about the Parsley fiasco, or this outrage would never have happened."

Clearly, something has fallen through the cracks. Clearly, Tool has failed to keep management properly informed.

Office Dartboard Insert

Jerry Malaria

You're standing in front of the coffee machine at 3:30. It's time for your afternoon shot of caffeine. Suddenly there's an annoying buzz in your ear.

"Psst! Hey! You're not going to believe this!"

You look down at the floor, hoping the buzz will go away. It doesn't. Your colleague Jerry Malaria is standing between you and your office. You're trapped. The buzzing gets more intense:

"You see the group of Chinese come in this morning? They're in with Dumpling. I heard a high-level exec say they're going to take us over. Banzai! Wouldn't it be just like those bastards to sell us out? We're the ones to suffer—the Big Guys will cut a great deal for themselves and leave us all to the dogs. You've got to be an idiot to stick around [trying to imitate a Japanese bow] Ahhhhh, So!"

Modus Operandi

Is anything Jerry says true? No. But it sure sounds like the truth. Jerry will cite 10 impeccable sources for each particle of mutilated information he disseminates. His rumors can neither be proven nor disproven; there's no way you can fact-check them, because Jerry's "impeccable" sources are always people in higher positions whom no one has ever met. Has Jerry met them? No, but he's pretty damned sure he knows what they're thinking!

Favorite Sayings

"We're going to get 1% raises again this year—while the big boys pull in the big bucks. Just wait and see."

"The only reason the boss got his job is because he married the CEO's niece."

"Be careful with your administrative assistant. They say you're spending too much on her overtime."

"I hope I'm not being insensitive: The boss thinks you need a social life."

"One of the Big Guys told me that we'll have some major changes. *Major* changes."

"Well there are going to be five promotions. I got three of the names from HR. The usual incompetent jerks. Don't feel bad if you get passed over."

"This business sucks. This department sucks. This company sucks. *Doesn't it?*"

"Good-bye, guys. Management is transferring me to a new division that specializes in dealing only with customers it considers important."

He's contagious. If you say a thing in response, he'll be sure to mutilate it and broadcast the result to the rest of the office, with attribution.

Office Dartboard Insert

Chuck Yeast

It's the face you see every day. It seems to come with the building. It's totally bland and doesn't have a name you can ever recall. And you're never sure what it's responsible for, or even what department it's attached to. And yet, no matter how much you move up or around in the company, that face is always there too.

Chuck Yeast.

How does he survive? How does he succeed?

- It can't be his management style; no one remembers working for him.
- It can't be his performance; he's never done anything that anyone can recall.
- It can't be his contacts; his father's not the CEO, and he's afraid of talking with any superiors for longer than 3 minutes.

Modus Operandi

He tunes in completely to what senior management wants from minute to minute, and he adjusts his career path accordingly. Is the executive suite pushing new office cubicles, Genetic Philanthropy, TotalNightVision 2020, Logo Management?

He *gets with* the program.

Chuck Yeast specializes in reading the handwriting on the wall. When his position or department is in jeopardy, he's the first one to sense it. And he's got a great system for managing career risk:

- If the boss wants it—no problem—do it immediately.
- If the boss wants it and it's a risk—no problem—assign it to a subordinate immediately.
- If the boss wants *him* to do it, and it's a risk—no problem—he will transfer to another division.

Yeast keeps a running list of every vacant executive slot throughout the entire corporation and can make good his escape within days. The slots on his list are ones that no one has ever heard of:

- Lobby Access Executive.
- Input Manager.
- Pacific Rim Liaison.

These positions are in departments that nobody understands:

- Variable Cost Aggregation.
- Trans-National Automation Services.
- Administration.

Yes, that's right. Chuck Yeast subtracts from the sum total of all corporate productivity.

Yeast doesn't care if nobody understands what he does. He's got the long view. He knows that in today's organization, the most competent performers have opinions, make noise, and attract attention—mostly by trying to do business. So, they all get fired. Chuck Yeast's objective is to not get fired.

Since nobody knows who he is, and nobody knows what he does, nobody makes the effort to get rid of him. He's here to stay.

Favorite Sayings

"July 4th occurs on a Wednesday this year."

"It's raining."

"Beef stroganoff in the cafeteria today."

"I don't know. I didn't hear the speech. I was up with Accounting."

"I can't make an exception. Those are the rules."

"But there is a way to get it done if you want. Board approval."

"The men's room is down the hall, second door on the right."

Office Dartboard Insert

Max Pilfer

It's a Jungle in Here

Max Pilfer has arrived at the conclusion that the competition isn't outside the building—like Brand X—but rather inside the building—people like you. He works on two principles: (a) to get ahead, everyone else has to get fired; and (b) he can generate more business by taking it from somebody else than by developing customers himself.

Modus Operandi

What Pilfer does to his colleagues:

- Never allows anyone to spend more time in the office than he does. If you make it in earlier, he will stay later, and come in yet earlier the next morning.
- Listens to every conversation in the office but pretends not to.
- Highlights his accomplishments by comparing them to the clearly inferior performance of colleagues like you.
- Tells subordinates how not to behave, using you as an example.
- Points the finger when a crisis occurs before anyone else knows it's a crisis.
- Gives your name and phone number to 10 or 12 insurance agents, 7 or 8 charities, 3 or 4 stockbrokers, multiple credit card issuers, and at least two accident lawyers.
- Routinely corrupts, moves, and/or deletes your data files on the shared drive. Pilfer knows exactly which of your files are critical.

How Pilfer gets business:

- Pilfer informally stretches the definition of his sales territory. He is responsible for the land transportation industry? He decides that railroads, car companies, and trucking firms aren't sufficient. Roller skates have wheels, don't they? So do scooters, bicycles, Playskool toys, and electric trains. Toy makers, toy retailers, and mass merchandisers are simply a natural extension of land transportation. These are supposed to be your customers, but he'll put them all in his budget. How are you going to find out? You won't, not until he's already booked a sale to them.
- Pilfer peruses the financial media for news about your customers. He emails the articles to the boss and the boss's boss with his name attached. They'll think the customers belong to Pilfer. And, come the reorganization, they will.

- The bank you work for has just developed a new product. The chances are that it will be a runaway bestseller. The problem is that senior management doesn't want to sell more than $500 million of these products. So, who gets how much of the allocation? Pilfer won't wait. He'll take the whole thing and shadow allocate it to companies he's never even contacted.

What does Pilfer do with all the turf he steals from his colleagues? Nothing. He doesn't do anything. That's because he doesn't really know how to do business. And he doesn't have time to take care of the customers anyway. He's too busy grabbing more customers from his colleagues. So, the existing business just rots away.

Favorite Sayings

"G'morning."

"You look tired. Ill?"

"I heard last night that Kenya's in trouble. Your deal will tank unless you get export insurance. Don't worry. I already told the boss."

"You leaving now?" [Glances at watch.] "G'night."

Office Dartboard Insert

E. Bunsen Burner III

There's bound to be somebody in your division who shows up for work just as you're going down for your coffee break:

"Heard you guys did *some job* on Project Blue."

With E. Bunsen Burner III ("Bunnie" for short), what you see is what you get. He's a team player. He can afford to be. He is one of the Elect: He is made in the image and likeness of senior management. And he's been on the fast track since his first day at work when he left the office at 3 to play squash with the Chairman.

Modus Operandi

Bunnie is invisible before 10. He is also invisible between noon and 2:30. But he does everyone the favor of staying late every day, until 6 p.m. Bankers' hours in London. Diminished face time and productivity doesn't impede his career though; he moves right up the ranks ahead of everyone else anyway.

How does he get ahead of everyone else? To be sure, he does know quite a bit about business. His father's. And his father is a friend of the CEO.

Burner III is tall, white, blonde, and awfully nice. Bunnie is a hell of a great guy. He never gets bothered by anything. He never does anything wrong—that can't be blamed on someone else. He never does anything right that isn't rewarded. He never does anything that doesn't move him right up the corporate ladder. He gets invited to executive outings and knows senior management—and all their spouses—on a first-name basis. They all talk about what a great job he's doing.

If you're in the same division, it means that you'll do all his work, get blamed for his mistakes, and have your best work credited to him. Don't get too worked up about it, though. It could be worse: He *could* be your boss. And at some point, he *will* be.

Favorite Sayings

"Hey, champ. That's great!"

"Holy Smokerinos! Looks like I'm late again. Rough night. Guess I just can't handle Chairman Fizz's 40-year-old port. Let me at the Java!"

"We keep our work open, shared, transparent. Zero tolerance disconnect. Total Tolerance Security. Cutting edge in transparent. Global."

"Our group objective is to be a robust player on that gameboard."

"It will take a headset change."

"We're at the tipping point. We're totally quality managing. Commitment. We're telling you the truth."

"We must reallocate the robustness of the resources. East, West, North, South. Hemispheres. Leaning in. Global."

"Segmentation drives off our paradigm. West Hemisphere is having some drama, but South Hemisphere continues to be relevant. Good work."

"The game plan is to kick butt."

"And what's my response? I'm clapping. I'm saying Yes. *Yes*!!"

"We mean business! Let's crank."

"Global! The future is ours!"

THE SUBORDINATES

The important thing to remember about subordinates is that you can never give the good ones the compensation or the promotions they feel they deserve, and you can never give the bad ones the boot.

As a result, the good ones blame you for being stingy and unresponsive, and the bad ones blame you for being ineffective.

The good ones leave. The bad ones, of course, stay.

Keep an eye out for the bad ones. They are the only people in the building who can terminate your career faster than Wyatt Earp, the boss most likely to fire you.

Office Dartboard Insert

Tar Pit

Tar Pit is a battery of enthusiasm one minute, a sullen rag doll the next. He pounces on you every time you enter and leave your office. He peers into the opening when your office door is ajar. He waits outside the lavatory to talk.

What sort of thing does he need to say?

> "I used 20-pitch type on the Bacon project. Is that okay?"

And if he can't get hold of you at the office, he phones you at home during dinner or after you've gone to bed. What does he need you so desperately for?

> "Two of the people who failed the Housekeeping Project are division execs!"

Modus Operandi

He is very serious about his career, as he will often tell you:

- His first day on the job he asks you where he'll be in 5 years.
- His second day on the job, he tells you when he'll be taking his vacation days: the Friday after Thanksgiving, both sides of every 3-day weekend, and the last 2 weeks of the year.
- He tells you how important it is in his life to be the best.
- He tells you how many friends he's talked with who think you're the greatest.
- He tells you how quickly his friends are getting promoted.
- He tells you how important it is in his life to get the cubicle by the window.

He volunteers for 10 or 12 jobs at a time and doesn't complete most of them. The ones he does complete are all wrong. He gets stunned, dejected, and hurt when you criticize his work. He tries to make up for it:

- Volunteers to pick up your car, your coffee, and your laundry.
- Volunteers to fill out your budgets, expense forms, reports, and performance reviews.
- Calls you and your boss "Ms." or "Mister."

Favorite Sayings

"I'm really on board with the new project. Not like Barbara."

"Did you hear what happened in Chet Chedder's division? Two vice presidents were caught together in the 10th-floor men's room last night. Two guys! Security caught them. Chet was called into Frye's office. I saw him go in myself."

"Sir, everyone is upset about the workload, but it's Grouper who is really the most pissed off."

"Sir, I've got to apologize. The two vice presidents weren't guys. It was a guy and a girl."

"Did you know that they turn off the air conditioning here at 2 in the morning? It gets so hot, I almost can't get any work done."

"Sir, I've got to apologize. It wasn't in Chet Chedder's division. But I still saw Chet coming out of Frye's office. And he looked horrible!"

"Why did George get that [high visibility assignment, desk by the window, new laser printer]? I've been here longer!"

If you think he tells you a lot about everyone else, just imagine what he's telling them about you. After all, he has to have something to show for the weeks and months he spends dialing your cell phone and pacing the tiles in front of your office door.

Office Dartboard Insert

Boom-Boom

Boom-Boom is the one individual in the whole corporation whom everyone likes. He's a very happy guy. He is continually grinning, continually surrounded by people and noise, continually away from his desk when not on the phone, and generally hung over. Boom-Boom also likes everyone in the whole corporation. Everyone, that is, except you. You expect him to work.

Modus Operandi

- Out the door at 4 every day except Fridays in football season, when he doesn't show up for work at all.
- Streams movies and sporting events to his laptop all day.
- Runs the football and basketball pools.
- Celebrates everyone's birthday with cake at 3 p.m.
- Borrows money from everyone, including the administrative assistants.
- Hoots, howls, and cackles at odd times of the day.
- Mistakes your most important client for somebody else.
- Leaves zeroes off of critical numbers.
- Blames you for not explaining it properly.
- Leaves the whole thing for you to redo.
- Loses all the data you need to complete the project.
- Gets astonished when you give him a bad review.
- Denies to the death all the bad things you say about him.
- Steals your wastebasket one week. Steals your mouse the next. Regularly moves your potted palm.

That call you get at 4 in the morning, just before you have to make a major presentation? It's a friend of his inviting you to a party that's still going strong. They're having a great time and they don't want you to miss it.

Boom-Boom is consistent. Every deadline's a crisis; every deadline is missed; and he never lets it get to him. Boom-Boom doesn't have to let it get to him. He has a friend somewhere up there in the executive suite—like just about everybody else except you.

He's also great for morale. He's fun, he makes his colleagues look good, and he's not a threat.

Except when it's time for his raise. You give him the raise he deserves, i.e., none. He throws up his arms and calls you unfair. Then you get a red alert call from the executive suite telling you to give him the same raise you give your best subordinates. When you give it to him, it will drive all the other subordinates nuts. Which is *bad* for morale. They tell the whole building that you play favorites and don't know how to manage. So, you end up being seen as an unfair, cruel, and incompetent bastard who plays favorites and doesn't know how to manage. Plus, now you have enemies in the executive suite.

Favorite Sayings

"Sure, I'm on top of it."

"Gee, I'm sorry. I don't remember your saying anything about a deadline."

"It's in process."

"Geez, you never told me to do that."

"God, you should see the dog he's married to."

"Which budget?"

"But I emailed that I would be at the Masters next week."

"Okay, everybody, brewskis at Joe's, 5 o'clock."

"Hey, no fades! You coming or not?"

Office Dartboard Insert

Termite

Termite graduated summa cum laude in subjects like demography, tax accounting, meteorology, or hospitality. He did extracurricular work during college—ran a seminar on the utilities industry; analyzed inventory for a drug store in Poughkeepsie; and/or studied flight patterns at O'Hare.

Termite appears to be the subordinate you always wanted. He is neat, hardworking, on time, no complaints, never talks about others.

On the other hand, Termite never volunteers for anything, never makes a controversial decision, and never makes a mistake you can pin on him.

Modus Operandi

- Spends hours analyzing the new divisional seating chart to determine who's on the fast track.
- Develops an estimate of everyone's salary.
- Uses your office when you're out on a trip.
- Talks to your boss when you're out.
- Talks to your boss's boss when your boss is out.
- Stares at you when you try to correct his mistakes.
- Denies making the mistakes.
- Stares at you when you point out the areas in which he can improve.
- Denies he needs to improve.
- Uses your administrative assistant to format his resume.

Sure, it's nice to have a subordinate who actually has the tools to get the job done.

But whatever he's doing isn't for the greater glory of you, your department, or the business. He's doing it expressly to get ahead, and he's not going to waste any time getting to where he needs to go.

Not that he wants your job. He doesn't. He wants your boss's job. You're just in the way. Everything he works on is being copied to your boss, like his strategies for improving corporate communications, increasing productivity, raising prices, and eliminating layers of management. He's the guy who produces the program for slashing headcount in your department—starting with you. Just what your boss and your boss's boss want to hear.

The damage this subordinate does is invisible up until your job evaporates and your department implodes.

Favorite Sayings

"Company policy dictates it, ma'am. Handbook Section 3.B.2.C. You can eat breakfast at your desk up until 8:30 a.m."

"If you hadn't told me to change that assumption, it would have gotten done, and done right."

"You will recall that you didn't ask for that."

"That's not in line with what the CEO said at the annual meeting."

"It's in the left-hand drawer of his desk at the very back."

"The executives in the other divisions really work hard. Maybe that's why they can get good bonuses for their people."

"If you can't talk to your boss about my raise, ma'am, I will."

Office Dartboard Insert

UFO

It's a Jungle in Here

UFO sports a deceptively high IQ. She also has intellectual hobbies—botany, philosophy, applied mathematics, and Chinese economic theory. She's been out of college for at least 3 years but is seeing the world for the very first time.

Modus Operandi

- Wears inappropriate, ill-fitting clothes.
- Shows up at the office at odd hours on different days.
- Spends hours browsing websites that interest her.
- Spends weeks trying to figure out how her assignments fit into (a) the global economy, (b) the history of ethics, or (c) the solar system.
- Phones people all over the organization at random to survey them on how they fit in.
- Ponders the question: "If your personal tax return is numbered 1040, shouldn't we know what is in forms 1039 and 1041?"
- Phones her parents at least twice a week.
- Shows up for work late because she had to stay up and watch (a) barn owl migrations, (b) the stock market open in Tokyo, or (c) a rebroadcast of Wagner's *Ring of the Nibelung*.
- Gets up and leaves in the middle of the divisional budget meeting. She doesn't come back because, as she later reports, she "needed to research some of the brilliant ideas that came up during the meeting."
- Gets new clothing and home appliances delivered to the office.
- Writes emails concerning your biggest customers and projects, and copies your boss and the CEO.
- Zeroes in on the least important part of every assignment.
- Gets overwhelmed by the deeper complexities she uncovers.
- Gives the assignment back to you at the end of the month, unfinished, in the form of 50 pages of unorganized notes and diagrams.
- Asks you to please explain the part of the assignment she didn't understand.
- Thinks your solution to the problem is much too simplistic.
- Stares at the floor when you tell her that her work is substandard.
- Gets hives.
- Phones people all over the organization at random to see what they think of your comments.
- Phones her parents.

UFO is always there when a crisis occurs. Even if she didn't create it, she'll work furiously to resolve it. Which guarantees it will get a lot worse.

You never know where she's coming from. She never knows where she is. But there's one thing for sure: She has a desk and a telephone in your department. And that's all the dynamite she needs. Since she feels just as comfortable phoning the chairman of the board as calling her sister in Denver, you'll be deluged with calls from incredulous superiors demanding immediate answers to programs, products, and events you know nothing about.

She's the only force in your whole department who has the capacity to commit minor errors and, through earnest and enthusiastic endeavor, blow them up into truly stupendous blunders.

How did she get there? How does she survive? Well, as you know, there are a bunch of people related to someone in the executive suite. She's one of them. Just grin and bear it.

Favorite Sayings

"This project is just like my senior thesis. Which is great because I got an 'A' on it."

"This project may be a bit much too advanced at this point in my career. But maybe in 2 or 3 months, I'll have learned enough to try it again."

"Why are the walls on the office cubicles only 4 feet high?"

"It's almost done. I haven't done the PowerPoint yet, but I've got it very clear in my head."

"When they reorganized, shouldn't they have put the Foreign Exchange Department in the International Division?"

"Why are there empty slots on the org chart?"

"I think I understand the issues better than anyone else on the floor. It's just that you're not making the best use of my talent."

"I've decided to help the Purchasing Department develop a just-in-time process. I know it's not in my work plan, but they clearly need to try it out."

"I called the president's office to suggest that he put the Foreign Exchange Department in the International Division."

"I called the CEO's office to let him know that the just-in-time process in Purchasing is exactly like what he described in his policy memo."

Office Dartboard Insert

Affidavit

It's a Jungle in Here

Affidavit lives in a world in which he or she is always being mistreated. He/she is always unhappy and always making subtle threats, the sort that can result in a suit against the company, the industry, the regulatory authorities, and you, his/her boss. Yet, Affidavit has no real cause for complaint and has never been mistreated. Affidavit is a serial plaintiff who knows all the words that will send you flying to HR for protection. Affidavit's constant indignation prevents him/her from accomplishing much in the way of work. Your time with the head of HR does the same for you.

Modus Operandi

- Can recite the laws against discrimination relevant to his or her gender, race, religion, age, sexual orientation, physical or mental limitations, national origin, and body type.
- Memorizes the entire company code of conduct.
- Before accepting a job offer, analyzes the details of every corporate benefit.
- Has an employment lawyer on speed dial.
- Retains his/her uncle as a medical doctor in case there is a need for an excuse to miss work.
- Subscribes to the Mayo Clinic and National Institutes of Health newsletters to be current on the symptoms of various illnesses.
- Puts the holidays for the world's religions on the work calendar and observes them all; dares anyone to protest it.
- Calls Security if someone lobs a paper clip in his/her direction.

Favorite Sayings:

"Your edits are abusive!"

"I can't help it. I suffer from extreme verbosity. It's real. Check the DSM."

"I dunno. I just feel, well, uncomfortable around my boss."

"I am being mistreated."

"I can't come back to the office yet. I had surgery on just the first bunion. After I recover, I'll go in for the second."

"Am I different in some way from the people who get invited to lunch with the division head? You know what I mean."

"Why does your secretary need access to our work calendars? This is becoming a-a-a hostile environment!"

"Got sick right after I got home from vacation. Turista, they call it. Will email again when I'm feeling better."

"I heard an off-color joke in the seventh-floor bathroom. How do I report it?"

"I was technically no longer on vacation as of the evening I landed back home, day before last. So yesterday was a sick day—*not* another vacation day. That's clearly the intent of the vacation policy."

"How old is your replacement? Younger than me, I'll bet."

"What is our compensation breakdown by age, gender, and race?"

"This company honors a different national origin each month—except for mine. When will we have Iceland month?"

"What??!!! How can our insurance company put me on disability after only 6 weeks out? Bunion surgery is serious! It's lucky I'm well. Yeah, I'll be back tomorrow. But the State Insurance Commissioner will hear from me!"

"I got a mediocre annual appraisal after asking for a compensation breakdown. Was that a coincidence?"

"My boss said I couldn't take time out for post-partum depression because it was my wife who was pregnant, not me. Well who's supposed to take care of her?"

"He touched my side of the table while we were talking. That's contrary to our values."

"Here's the extension of someone in Employee Relations. She wants to talk to you."

Laws governing discrimination, bias, and harassment are there to redress the inequities and injustices inflicted on generations of people who work for a living. Affidavit knows how to play the game and is happy to do so, at the cost of trivializing what are genuine problems for others in the workforce. He/she thinks that the ever-present threat of a lawsuit from one of his/her many complaints will prevent firing, even when he/she doesn't do the job. This MO dramatically raises the compensation per hour worked.

Was he/she a middle child who has always felt he/she was treated unfairly? Or does he/she think the company will cough up $5 million for him/her to go away? No matter the reason, you had better bone up on employment law, tropical diseases, and whatever pride-emerging or separatist cultures—Slavic? Celt-Iberian? Hillbilly? Hottentot?—that Affidavit is likely to trace his/her DNA back to.

YIKES!!!

No wonder everybody thinks American managers are the best in the world!

Look at the whack-jobs we have to deal with!

And we still get the job done!